P9-DYP-708

TRUE or FALSE?

This photo of a water park was taken from a traffic helicopter about 1,500 feet (457 m) above the ground.

FALSE!

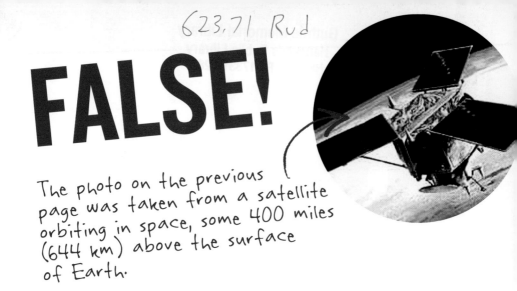

The photo on the previous page was taken from a satellite orbiting in space, some 400 miles (644 km) above the surface of Earth.

These days, there are thousands of satellites circling Earth. Some transmit radio and TV shows. Others are used for navigation or research. And some are used for spying.

To find out more about what's up there looking down at us, keep reading!

Book design Red Herring Design/NYC

Library of Congress Cataloging-in-Publication Data
Rudy, Lisa Jo, 1960–
Eyes in the sky : satellite spies are watching you! / by Lisa Jo Rudy.
    p. cm. — (24/7: Science Behind the Scenes)
Includes bibliographical references and index.
ISBN-13: 978-0-531-12082-8 (lib. bdg.)   978-0-531-18732-6 (pbk.)
ISBN-10: 0-531-12082-1 (lib. bdg.)   0-531-18732-2 (pbk.)
1. Space surveillance—Juvenile literature. I. Title.
UG1520.R83 2007
623'.71—dc22   2006005870

Published simultaneously in Canada. Printed in the United States of America.

SCHOLASTIC, FRANKLIN WATTS, and associated logos are trademarks and/or registered trademarks of Scholastic Inc.
1 2 3 4 5 6 7 8 9 10   R   17 16 15 14 13 12 11 10 09 08

EYES IN THE SKY

Satellite Spies Are Watching You!

Lisa Jo Rudy

WARNING: Okay, okay, so satellites probably aren't watching *you*. But satellites are getting more and more sophisticated. Right now, they can identify objects much smaller than a compact car. So if the thought of countries spying on each other from space bothers you, this book is *not* for you.

Franklin Watts
An Imprint of Scholastic Inc.
New York • Toronto • London • Auckland • Sydney
Mexico City • New Delhi • Hong Kong
Danbury, Connecticut

CONTENTS

TRUE-LIFE CASE FILES!

Real stories about spy satellites.

Sputnik was a little satellite that caused a big fuss.

15 Case #1:
First in Space

Americans were assuming that they'd be the first in space. Then they got a big surprise.

25 Case #2:
Project Corona

It seemed as though the U.S. spy satellite program was doomed to fail. But it became one of the great success stories of the Space Age.

The U.S. used this to spy on the U.S.S.R. from space.

UNITED

Colin Powell used satellite photos to make a case for war.

35 Case #3:
The Case of the Dictator's Weapons

Spy satellite photos showed what looked like biological and chemical weapons facilities in Iraq.

5

SPY DOWNLOAD

Peer down on this information about satellites.

YELLOW PAGES

There are more than 1,000 satellites orbiting Earth. Some are as small as melons. Others are as big as trucks.

SPY 411

Satellites relay TV, radio, and phone signals. They track weather systems and monitor environmental changes. They help people navigate. And they allow countries to spy on each other from above.

IN THIS SECTION:

▶ how satellite experts really talk;

▶ what famous landmarks look like from space;

▶ and where, exactly, all those satellites are.

Liftoff!

People who work with satellites have their own way of talking. Find out what their **vocabulary** means.

satellite
(SAT-uh-lite) a natural or human-made object that circles a planet, moon, or star

This is mission control. And it's liftoff for the rocket carrying our new satellite.

The rocket will release the satellite into orbit at noon.

orbit
(OR-bit) the path of a satellite around a planet, moon, or star

The satellite will begin to transmit images as soon as we run some tests on the cameras.

transmit
(transs-MIT) to send a message or radio signal from one place to another

We expect those images to provide new **intelligence** about our enemy's weapons systems.

intelligence
(in-TEL-uh-jens) secret information gathered by spies about another country's military and political plans and operations

The satellite will also do **reconnaissance** on troop movements in the area.

reconnaissance
(ree-KAHN-ah-sahns) the secret scouting or exploration of an area, usually for military or political purposes

Say What?

Here's some more lingo related to satellites and spying.

HUMINT
(HYOO-mint) information gathered by secret agents and spies. HUMINT is short for *human intelligence.*

SIGINT
(SIG-int) information gathered by intercepting communications such as radio and phone transmissions. SIGINT is short for *signal intelligence.*
*"You need spies in place to get **HUMINT**, but **SIGINT** can be gathered from far away."*

IMINT
(IH-mint) getting information from satellite photos or other kinds of images. IMINT is short for *imagery intelligence.*

resolution
(rez-uh-LOO-shuhn) the level of detail that can be seen in a photo
*"Today's best **IMINT** satellites have a **resolution** of about six inches (15.2 cm). They can spot a newspaper on the ground but can't read the headline."*

Out of This World

There are many kinds of satellites. And some of them are pretty good photographers.

A satellite is any object that travels around another one in space. Earth is a satellite of the Sun. And the Moon is a satellite of Earth.

The Moon is Earth's only *natural* satellite. But there are thousands of human-made satellites circling the planet.

Some satellites are for communication. They relay TV, radio, and phone signals.

Others are used by scientists to study Earth's oceans and **atmosphere**, or to forecast the weather.

Global Positioning System (**GPS**) satellites help people navigate and make maps.

Imaging satellites take pictures of the world below. Spy satellites take reconnaissance photos—but they're top secret.

These photos were taken by imaging satellites. Which famous landmarks and events do you recognize?

Answers: 1–Niagara Falls; 2–Pyramids of Giza; 3–Statue of Liberty; 4–Hurricane Katrina; 5–U.S. Capitol; 6–Golden Gate Bridge; 7–Mt. Everest; 8–The Pentagon; 9–NYC on 9/11.

5

4

6

Here are some satellite photos of famous landmarks and events. Which do you recognize?

STATUE OF LIBERTY · GOLDEN GATE BRIDGE · MOUNT EVEREST · NIAGARA FALLS · THE PENTAGON · PYRAMIDS OF GIZA · NYC ON 9/11 · HURRICANE KATRINA BEARING DOWN ON NEW ORLEANS · U.S. CAPITOL

7

9

8

The Satellite Team

It takes a lot of people to build, launch, and operate a satellite.

MISSION CONTROLLERS
These are the people who plan the missions and operate the satellites. Controllers at the National Reconnaissance Office (NRO) are in charge of all U.S. spy satellites.

LAUNCH TEAMS
Rocket scientists design the powerful rockets that carry satellites into orbit. Large teams of engineers and mechanics are responsible for launching them.

SATELLITES
Satellites are high-tech, robotic instruments that are sent into space. They are then operated remotely from hundreds, or even thousands, of miles away.

ENGINEERS AND TECHNICIANS
They design and build satellites and their power, control, and communication systems.

SCIENTISTS
Many scientists use satellites to observe and study Earth's climate, oceans, and environment. Other scientists get data from satellites that peer into deep space.

INTELLIGENCE ANALYSTS
The National Geospatial-Intelligence Agency (NGA) analyzes spy satellite imagery and prepares intelligence reports for the government.

TRUE-LIFE

CASE FILES!

24 hours a day, 7 days a week, 365 days a year, satellites are spying on the world below.

IN THIS SECTION:

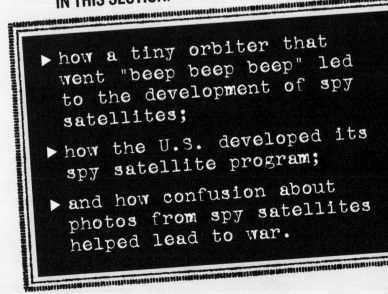

- ▶ how a tiny orbiter that went "beep beep beep" led to the development of spy satellites;

- ▶ how the U.S. developed its spy satellite program;

- ▶ and how confusion about photos from spy satellites helped lead to war.

Around the World in 90 Minutes

How high above us are satellites? It all depends on what their purpose is.

Low Earth Orbit (LEO)

Satellites in LEO are 150 to 500 miles (241 to 805 km) above us. It takes them about 90 minutes to complete one orbit. Many imaging and spy satellites are put in LEO so their cameras can get a close look at Earth. The space shuttle also uses a low earth orbit.

Polar Orbit

Some weather and Earth observation satellites are in low orbits that take them across both the North Pole and the South Pole. Satellites in polar orbit can see almost any spot on Earth.

Geostationary Orbit (GEO)

A satellite in GEO (22,300 miles or 35,900 km away) circles Earth in a west-to-east direction once every 24 hours. In this orbit, a satellite remains fixed over the same spot on Earth. TV satellites are in geostationary orbit. People who get satellite TV aim their dishes directly at one of these satellites.

In 1957, Americans could see a Russian satellite crossing the sky.

First in Space

Americans were assuming that they would be the first in space. Then they got a big surprise.

A Superpower's Superpowers

The only thing the first satellite could do was go "beep, beep, beep."

Imagine being able to see through clouds. Or being able to spot a football from hundreds of miles below. Or listening in on conversations on the other side of the planet.

Comic book heroes aren't the only ones with superpowers. U.S spy satellites can do all those things—and more.

That wasn't always the case. Earlier spy satellites could only take pictures.

And the very first satellite couldn't even do that. All it did was go "beep, beep, beep."

Still, its launch was one of the biggest events of the 20th century. And it came as a complete surprise.

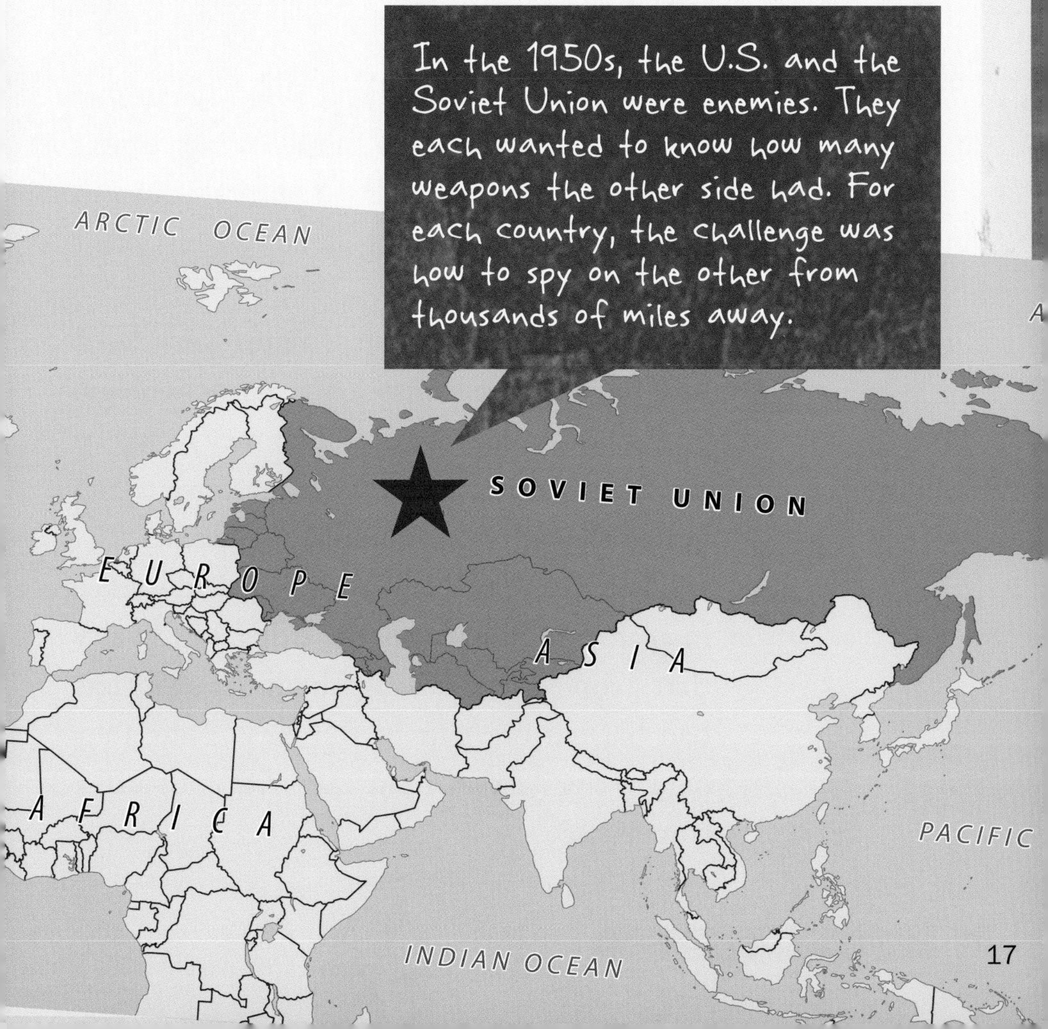

In the 1950s, the U.S. and the Soviet Union were enemies. They each wanted to know how many weapons the other side had. For each country, the challenge was how to spy on the other from thousands of miles away.

ARCTIC OCEAN

SOVIET UNION

EUROPE

ASIA

AFRICA

PACIFIC

INDIAN OCEAN

Soaring into Space

The launch of *Sputnik* was a triumph for the Soviet Union—and a major blow to America's confidence.

It was Friday, October 4, 1957. People were looking forward to the weekend. The big topic of conversation was the World Series. The Milwaukee Braves and the New York Yankees were tied at one game apiece.

But by Saturday morning, baseball had been pushed from the front pages by breaking news. America's rival, the **Soviet Union**, had launched the world's first satellite. It was called *Sputnik*.

"Up Goes a Man-Made Moon," read one headline. "Russia Wins the Race into Outer Space" read another. For the first time in history, a human-made object was in orbit around the planet.

At the time, the United States considered itself the world leader in science and **technology**. So Americans had assumed that they would be the first to reach space. Now the Soviets had beaten them. It was a humiliating defeat.

That Saturday, New York beat Milwaukee in Game 3. But it was the other big rivalry that people were talking about. The Soviets had blasted one out of the park. Now they held a big lead. Could the U.S. pull off a comeback?

A New Age Begins

Sputnik was about the size of a basketball. How could something so small cause such a big fuss?

Sputnik was a small metal ball that weighed 184 pounds (83 kg). It traveled 17,000 miles per hour (27,360 kph) and circled the world once every 96 minutes. As it passed by 550 miles (885 km) overhead, it sent out a radio signal.

Radio operators picked up *Sputnik*'s "beep, beep, beep" sound. TV stations played it over and over. One announcer described it as "the sound that . . . separates the old from the new." The Space Age had begun.

Americans were stunned by news of the *Sputnik* launch. Bill Foley, a writer for the *Florida Times-Union*, remembered the event this way: "The reaction throughout the United

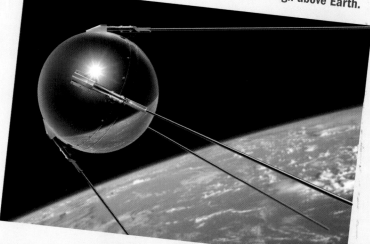

This drawing shows *Sputnik* in orbit high above Earth.

States was universal: We're all gonna die."

Foley was exaggerating. But it is true that the little satellite scared many Americans. Some thought it was a new kind of space weapon or spying device.

Most people, however, realized that *Sputnik* itself was harmless. Still, they were frightened by what it meant. Up until then, nobody was sure if the Soviets had **missiles** that could reach the U.S. Now they knew the Soviets had a rocket powerful enough to carry a satellite into space. That meant they could build missiles capable of hitting American cities. And those missiles could carry **nuclear weapons**.

Americans' greatest fear at the time was the possibility of a surprise nuclear attack. Now that the Soviets had the ability to strike at the U.S from far away, would they do it?

A group of Soviet missiles. With the launch of *Sputnik* in 1957, it was clear that the Soviet Union had missiles that could reach the U.S.

A Second Surprise

The Soviets launch another satellite. And this one has a passenger.

Americans were in for another shock. A month later, the Soviets launched *Sputnik 2*. It carried a dog named Laika. By sending a living creature into space, the Soviets had scored another first.

They had also managed to give Americans another scare. *Sputnik 2* was bigger than *Sputnik*. It had taken even more rocket power to carry this satellite into space. There was no longer any doubt that Soviet missiles could reach the U.S.

The Soviet leader Nikita Khrushchev boasted that the *Sputniks* were proof that his country was ahead of the U.S. in science and technology. He even predicted that the Soviet Union would be the first country to land on the Moon.

Once again, American pride had been badly damaged, and people looked to the government for answers. A satellite program had been in the works for several years. What was taking so long?

Laika was the first living creature to go into space. Here, the dog is shown resting inside *Sputnik 2* before the satellite was launched. Laika died in space.

RACING TO SPACE

Why were the U.S. and the Soviet Union in a space race, anyway?

Starting in the 1950s, the Soviet Union and the United States were in a race to reach space. Why was it so important to be first?

A major part of the space race was about military power. Leaders from each country dreamed of spying from space— and maybe even of attacking from space.

Another part of the race was about scientific knowledge. Most everyone agreed that exploring space would lead to scientific discoveries about Earth and the solar system. Each side wanted that knowledge first.

Communism vs. Democracy

The race was also about political differences. The Soviet Union and the U.S. had totally different kinds of governments. The Soviet Union was a **communist** state. Its government controlled most aspects of people's lives. The U.S. is a **democracy** whose citizens can make many of their own choices.

Both countries wanted to prove that their system was the best. One way to do that was to show off their scientific successes. And few things would impress the world as much as launching a satellite into space.

Soviets in First Place

The Soviets won the first round. But who won the race? In 1969, the U.S. took the lead when Neil Armstrong stepped onto the surface of the Moon. But the Soviets also had many firsts.

Today, the two countries are no longer rivals. In fact, these days, astronauts from Russia (which was part of the Soviet Union) and the U.S. work side by side on the International Space Station.

U.S. astronaut Buzz Aldrin was the second human to set foot on the moon, in 1969. Aldrin was part of the *Apollo 11* mission, when astronaut Neil Armstrong became the first human on the moon.

The U.S. Evens the Score

A tiny satellite restores American pride.

After *Sputnik*, the American satellite program kicked into high gear. The project had made already made a lot of progress. But technical and political issues had slowed it down.

The first launch took place on December 6, 1957. TV cameras from around the world were there. But the rocket only got a few feet off the ground before exploding. The reporters weren't kind. One headline mocked, "Oh, What a Flopnik!"

The second attempt to launch a satellite also failed. But on January 31, 1958, *Explorer 1* reached orbit. It was much smaller than *Sputnik*, but Americans were relieved and happy to finally have a satellite in space.

Vanguard 1 was the second U.S. satellite to reach orbit. It weighed only three pounds (1.4 kg). The tiny satellite is still circling Earth.

The U.S and the Soviets went on to launch many more satellites in the coming years. They were bigger than the first ones, and their instruments were more sophisticated. But none ever captured the world's attention as much as the *Sputniks* and *Explorer 1*.

The Next Step: Spying from Space

A few months after the launch of *Explorer 1*, President Dwight Eisenhower gave the go-ahead for an ambitious new project. Its goal was to build a satellite that could **spy** on the Soviet Union.

The U-2 flew spying missions over the Soviet Union. The plane's first fight was in 1955.

The U.S. had been using a spy plane called the U-2 to take photos of Soviet airfields and missile sites. The U-2 was providing valuable intelligence. But it could only cover a small area at a time. And even though it flew very high, there was always the possibility that it would be shot down.

Satellites could not be shot down. And their cameras could cover a much greater area. But getting a spy satellite into orbit would turn out to be much harder than anyone expected. 24/7

The next case tells more about how the U.S. took its rivalry with the Soviet Union into outer space.

Project Corona

Transports

It seemed as though the U.S. spy
satellite program was doomed to
fail. But it became one of the great
success stories of the Space Age.

Bombers

A Top-Secret Project

Spy satellites gave U.S. leaders the best view they'd ever had of what the enemy was doing.

U-2 pilot Gary Powers was captured by the Soviets in 1960. He was convicted of spying and sentenced to prison. The Soviets released Powers after 21 months.

May 1, 1960 was a dark day for the **CIA**. American pilot Gary Powers had been shot down as he flew a U-2 spy plane over the Soviet Union.

U.S. president Dwight Eisenhower grounded all U-2 planes. That left the spy agency with no eyes in the sky. **Aerial** reconnaissance was the best way for the U.S. to spy on its enemy, the Soviet Union. The U-2s could monitor how strong the Soviet's military was. Without these planes, Eisenhower said, he felt "blind."

Fortunately, the CIA and the Air Force had another plan. For years, they had been trying to get a spy satellite into orbit. That project was codenamed Corona.

Corona had run into a lot problems. But on August 18, just months after the U-2 crash, the first Corona satellite began snapping pictures of the Soviet Union. They were the first photos ever taken from space. And they covered a much bigger area than the cameras on a U-2 ever could.

Over the next 12 years, Corona satellites gave American leaders the ability to learn a lot about the secretive Soviet Union. But only a few people were able to celebrate when those first photos came in. The Corona spy satellite program was top secret. It would remain secret for the next 35 years.

Who Has More Missiles?

People in both the U.S. and the Soviet Union lived in fear of a surprise nuclear attack.

President Eisenhower had approved the Corona project back in 1958. At the time, the United States and the Soviet Union were in an **arms race**. Each side wanted to make sure it had more arms— weapons—than the other.

The Soviet leader Nikita Khrushchev often boasted that his country was winning the arms race. He bragged that Soviet factories were churning out nuclear missiles "like sausages."

The idea that the Soviets had more

Khrushchev frightened Americans with his claims that the Soviet Union had more missiles than the U.S.

missiles than the U.S. terrified Americans. But was it true? Was there really a gap between how many missiles the U.S. had and how many the Soviets had? Eisenhower had to find out if this missile gap really existed. He needed numbers.

And the only way to count missile sites was from the air. So when the Air Force proposed the Corona project in February 1958, Eisenhower quickly gave it the okay.

"A Most Heartbreaking Business"

For a long time, it seemed like the Corona project was doomed to failure.

The team chosen to build the first spy satellite faced big challenges. They had to design a camera that could take pictures from 100 miles (160 km) above Earth. The team also had to figure how to get the actual film from these cameras back home. (At the time, there wasn't any technology for transmitting images electronically.)

They also had to keep the Soviets from finding out about the project. That wasn't going to be easy. To get a satellite into space, you have to launch it from a rocket. And rocket launches are visible from miles away.

Rocket launches are loud and fiery; they can't be kept secret.

Officials at the Air Force realized that it would be impossible to keep Corona secret. So they came up with a cover story. They announced the "Discoverer" project. They said that the purpose of Discoverer was to gather scientific information.

Americans greeted the news of this project with excitement. Ever since *Sputnik*, Americans had been obsessed with space.

The so-called *Discoverer 1* was launched in February 1959. It went into orbit—but it was just a test flight. Then the next 11 launches were all failures. Sometimes the rockets misfired or the satellites entered the wrong orbit.

The team had come up with a clever—but complicated—way to recover the film. After the camera in the satellite took pictures, the satellite would **eject** a **capsule** containing the used film. That capsule was equipped with a heat shield that would keep it from burning up as it traveled through the atmosphere. The capsule also had a parachute that would slow its fall once it got near Earth.

The final step invloved using a plane to snatch the capsule out of the air. It was a complex process, and many things could go wrong. And it seemed like they all did.

The team experienced one setback after another for 18 months. "[It was] a most heartbreaking business," project director Richard Bissell admitted later. "And it went on and on." Bissell kept everyone's spirits up by reminding them they were attempting to do something that had never been done before. Finally, in August 1960, things began to go right.

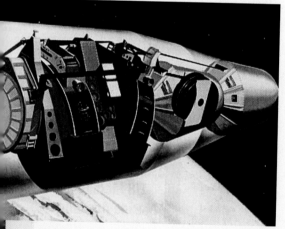

This painting shows a Corona project satellite in orbit. It was a huge challenge to design and launch a satellite that could take photos from space.

14th Time Is a Charm

The team's determination and hard work finally began to pay off.

Discoverer 13 was successfully launched on August 10. It passed repeatedly over the Soviet Union. And the film capsule was safely ejected. But clouds made it hard for a plane to catch it in midair. Instead, the capsule splashed down in the Pacific Ocean. It was quickly recovered by a helicopter.

There was no film in it since the mission was designed only to test the capsule recovery system. Still, it was the first time a human-made object had ever been returned from space. The team finally had something to celebrate.

President Eisenhower (*right*) called the *Discoverer 13* mission "historic." Here he looks at a flag that was carried back to Earth in the return capsule (*left*).

Discoverer 14 blasted into space on August 18. Its camera took thousands of photos of Soviet military sites. Captain Harold Mitchell, a pilot from the Air Force, was back in the air, waiting. He had missed the capsule on August 10. But this time he felt optimistic. In fact, when he'd left the house that morning, he'd told his wife, "I'll get it this time, honey."

A rig that looked like a circus trapeze hung below his plane. It consisted of two long poles with a rope and hook stretched

31

An Air Force plane caught the capsule ejected from the satellite by hooking the capsule's parachute.

between them. Mitchell's job was to fly over the capsule and snag its parachute with the hook. But first he had to locate the capsule.

Suddenly Mitchell spotted its brightly colored parachute in the distance. He turned the plane toward it.

Mitchell missed his first pass by a few inches. He turned the plane and made another approach, but missed again. The capsule was falling fast, and Mitchell knew he had only one chance left. He flew directly over the parachute, and this time he hooked it. "That's it!" a crewman called. "You've got a hold of it."

"I was so nervous I could hardly handle it," Mitchell told reporters when he landed. His midair catch made headlines the next day. The articles reported that the capsule's scientific instruments were undamaged. Nobody knew that it also contained top-secret film.

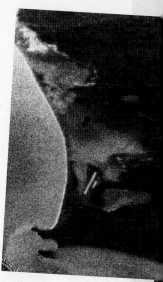

Discoverer 14 took this photo of a Soviet air base from 100 miles (160 km) above Earth. It was the first photo ever taken by a spy satellite.

The film from *Discovery 14* was quickly developed. CIA officials were thrilled by what they saw. The satellite had taken pictures of more Soviet area than all the U-2 flights combined. The U.S. now had a brand-new way to spy on the Soviets from above.

A History of Success

Corona provided leaders with valuable intelligence for many years.

Over the next 12 years, 145 Corona satellites were launched. Their cameras took more than 800,000 pictures. U.S. leaders gained important intelligence about the Soviet Union's weapons from the photos. And they discovered that Khrushchev had been faking. He had far fewer missiles than the United States—not more.

Lyndon B. Johnson became president in 1963. He later described the great value of the spy satellite project to the U.S. It showed that "we were harboring fears that we didn't need to have." The intelligence gathered by the satellites allowed him to make decisions based on hard facts, not on wild guesses.

In the 1990s, Vice President Al Gore pushed for Corona photos to be made public. He knew the photos could help environmentalists learn how Earth's surface has changed.

By 1972, new imaging technologies made it possible to transmit photos electronically. It was no longer necessary to retrieve film capsules. And it was time for a new generation of spy satellites.

The Corona project remained a secret until 1995. Today, everyone has access to photos taken by Corona satellites. Environmentalists study changes in the Earth's surface by comparing those images to more recent satellite photos.

What about today's U.S. spy satellites? The program is top secret and very little is known. According to some experts, the later Corona satellites could spot objects about six feet (1.8 m) wide. Today's spy satellites can probably see something as small as six inches (15.2 cm) wide.

Does that mean these spy satellites can see you? Yes and no. They can spot you standing outside your house—but they can't identify who you are. At least we don't *think* they can. But only the CIA knows for sure. 24/7

In the next case, find out how spy satellites helped make the case for a recent war.

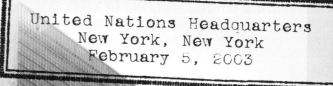

United Nations Headquarters
New York, New York
February 5, 2003

The Case of the Dictator's Weapons

Spy satellite photos showed what looked like biological and chemical weapons facilities in Iraq.

Preparing for War

Could the U.S. secretary of state convince other members of the United Nations to back the invasion of Iraq?

The grand chamber was hushed as U.S. Secretary of State Colin Powell started to speak. "This is an important day for all of us," he said.

It was February 5, 2003, and Powell was addressing the **United Nations** Security Council. The Council is made up of representatives from 15 countries. Its job is to keep peace between nations.

The Security Council of the United Nations listened as Colin Powell made his case.

Powell had come to the U.N. to explain why the U.S. government was preparing to invade Iraq. He hoped to convince other nations to help the U.S. overthrow the leader of Iraq, Saddam Hussein.

Hussein was a brutal **dictator** who ruled by force and **intimidation**. Many Iraqis lived in fear. He mistreated people who did not belong to his religious group and political party. Sometimes he killed them. In one instance, Hussein's forces attacked a community of Kurds, a minority group. The forces used deadly **chemical weapons—nerve** and **mustard gas**. About 5,000 Kurdish men, women and children were killed.

Hussein had done terrible things to his

In 2003, world leaders debated whether there were still weapons of mass destruction in Iraq.

own people. President George W. Bush and his advisers believed that he was also a threat to other countries. They were convinced that he was hiding weapons of mass destruction (**WMD**s) such as biological and chemical weapons. These weapons spread toxins or disease-carrying germs. They can kill thousands of people at a time.

The administration also believed that Hussein was developing nuclear weapons.

"There is no doubt that Hussein now has weapons of mass destruction," Vice President Dick Cheney had said in a speech. "There is no doubt that he is amassing them to use against our friends, against our **allies**, and against us."

Saddam Hussein took part in overthrowing the government in Iraq in 1968. He became president in 1979.

Hussein claimed that Iraq had destroyed its WMDs years ago. But President Bush and many other people said they didn't believe him. They decided it was time to get rid of Hussein. And that meant going to war.

Powell knew that many members of the U.N. Security Council doubted that Iraq still had WMDs. But he was about to show them new proof that they did exist. By sharing that information, Powell felt he could convince other countries to support the U.S.-led invasion.

Powell told the Security Council members that he had important intelligence about Iraq to share with them.

Making His Case

Powell uses photos taken by spy satellites to support his argument.

"My colleagues," Powell began, "every statement I make today is . . . based on solid intelligence." That intelligence came from many sources, he said. Some came from **bugged** phone conversations. Some came from Iraqi citizens. Powell said that these Iraqis "have risked their lives to let the world

Powell showed this photo of a missile site in Iraq. He said it showed trucks moving missiles to hide them from U.N. inspectors.

know what Saddam Hussein is really up to."

And some intelligence came from spy satellites. Powell said that the satellite photos showed that chemical weapons were being moved from factories into the field.

Powell began showing satellite photos. "[Satellite photos] are hard for the average person to interpret, hard for me," he warned. He said that he had asked imagery specialists to tell him what the photos revealed. Imagery specialists are trained to interpret satellite photos.

The photos were aerial shots of buildings in Iraq. Powell said that these buildings were "associated with biological or chemical weapons activities." He went on to explain that photos of one site showed "active chemical munitions bunkers." Those are buildings used to store chemical weapons.

Photos of another site, Powell said, showed trucks used to carry chemical weapons. He also pointed to what he said was a "decontamination vehicle." The purpose of this truck was to clean up a spill if anything went wrong. That truck said a lot, Powell explained. It would only be there if chemical weapons were present.

Even so, Powell said that the photos by themselves did not provide enough proof. There were also **eyewitness** reports of "movement of chemical weapons" at the sites.

"It's not just the photo," Powell said. "It's the photo and then the knowledge of an individual being brought together to make the case."

Powell ended by saying that all the evidence proved that Hussein had WMDs. "Should we take the risk that he will not some day use these weapons?" he asked. No, he said. It was a risk the U.S. was not willing to take.

A month later, the U.S.-led invasion of Iraq began.

Powell said this satellite photo showed a building in which chemical weapons were stored.

10 Nov 2002

Decontamination Vehicle

Security

Chemical Munitions Bunker

SPYING ON THE WORLD

Very little is known about today's U.S. spy satellites.

U.S. intelligence services have fewer than 20 satellites in orbit. But little is known about their top-secret missions. Spy satellites can probably observe any spot on Earth at least once a day. These spy satellites are operated by the National Reconnaissance Office (**NRO**). The NRO releases almost no information about the satellites. "The less people know or think they know about what we have, [the better]," says NRO spokesperson Rick Oborn.

A Fruitless Search

Would the troops find WMDs hidden all over Iraq?

On March 20, a military force of 300,000 invaded Iraq. Of those, 98 percent were American and British troops. By early May, they controlled the capital city of Baghdad and some areas of the country. But no WMDs had been found.

There were no chemical or biological weapons at the buildings shown in the satellite photos. The trucks turned out to be fire engines and regular cargo haulers. And troops who searched hundreds of other sites found nothing. "They're simply not there," concluded Lieutenant General James T.

U.S. soldiers patrol the streets of Baghdad, the capital of Iraq.

After troops took control of Baghdad, this statue of Saddam Hussein was pulled down.

Conway, commander of the 1st Marine Expeditionary Force, in June.

Over the next few years, rebels stepped up attacks against U.S. forces. Various Iraqi groups took sides against each other. The country descended into **civil war**. Hussein was tracked down, tried, found guilty, and executed. A new government was put in place. But no WMDs were ever found. What had happened?

A Matter of Interpretation

It's not easy to interpret satellite photos and other intelligence.

It seems now that intelligence analysts looked at all the evidence they had gathered— and came to some incorrect conclusions.

To understand how that could have happened, imagine this scenario. Say you have to put together a puzzle of a painting by an artist you know a little about. You don't have the box the puzzle came in, so you don't know what the painting looks like. And what's more, you're missing a lot of puzzle pieces!

You put together all the pieces you have. Then you take a look. You can see that there are bits and pieces of people. They seem to be dancing. Or maybe they're fighting? You can't tell.

At this point, you could come up with a good guess about what's going on in the picture. Say you happen to know that the artist is famous for painting boxers. So you might decide that the people in this puzzle are fighting. It's a reasonable guess.

But you're not necessarily right. This could be the only painting the painter ever did of dancers.

Now, back to the intelligence analysts. They, too, have to look at many pieces of a puzzle. Some of the pieces are supplied by spies and eyewitnesses. Others come from bugs or surveillance cameras. And spy satellites provide important intelligence as well.

Fit together, these pieces form an incomplete picture. Imagery specialists and intelligence analysts then have to come up with some theories about what the picture shows.

In the case of the WMDs, there seems to have been many problems with figuring out what the picture showed. First, there were too many missing pieces of information. Second, some of the information was wrong. Many of the eyewitnesses in Iraq provided bad information.

And finally, much of the intelligence was misinterpreted. The analysts seem to have drawn the wrong conclusion about the big picture from the pieces of evidence.

Spy satellites have been great tools for the U.S. military during times of crisis. Still, no form of **espionage** is foolproof. Satellites can take photos of buildings and trucks. But they can't look inside them. Spies can listen in on people's private conversations. But they can't read their minds. **Informants** can describe what they've seen—or they can lie about it.

In the end, solid intelligence comes from good information plus accurate analysis of that information. And as this case shows, incorrect interpretations of information can have serious consequences. 24/7

SPY DOWNLOAD

Here's more amazing intelligence about satellites.

IN THIS SECTION:

▶ how spying from balloons led to modern aerial reconnaissance;

▶ why a satellite orbiting Mars made headlines;

▶ how space has become a junkyard;

▶ if working with satellites is the career for you!

1794 The First Spy in the Sky

The French army uses a reconnaissance balloon (*left*) to monitor the Austrian army during the Battle of Fleurus. That intelligence helps them win the battle.

Key Dates in

Armies have been looking down on their enemies for more than 200 years.

Aerial

1861 U.S. Army Balloon Corps

Thaddeus Lowe (*right*) convinces President Lincoln that balloons can help him win the Civil War. On September 24, Lowe goes up in a balloon 1,000 feet (305 m) above the ground. From there, he telegraphs information about distant Confederate troops to Union commanders. They are able to fire accurately at enemy troops—even though they can't see them. That's a first in military history. The Union's seven balloons contribute to some key victories.

1914—1918 Biplanes As Spy Planes

During World War I, both sides use biplanes (*left*) to scout enemy territory. The planes hold two people—the pilot and the observer. At first, the observers draw sketches of enemy positions. But soon they begin using cameras. Aerial photography is born.

1939—1945 World War II

Aerial reconnaissance (*right*) plays a major role in all military operations. Photography allows commanders to get a very clear picture of enemy activity. The scouting missions are dangerous, and many flying spies are shot down. Millions of photos are taken from the air.

1956—1960 U-2 Flies High

The **Cold War** is heating up, and the CIA needs a spy plane that can fly so high it can't be shot down. It builds the U-2, which flies at 70,000 feet (21 km), out of range of Soviet missiles. For four years, the U-2 gathers valuable intelligence about Soviet missile sites and weapons.

Reconnaissance

1959—1972 The First U.S. Spy Satellites

The U.S launches 145 Corona spy satellites. They give the government a much clearer picture of Soviet military power than it had ever had before (*below*). One Corona mission returns as many photos as all the U-2 flights put together.

1980s—present Seeing Through Clouds

Cameras can't see through clouds. So the U.S. develops radar imaging systems. Some of its satellites can now take photos no matter how bad the weather is. Others can "see" objects less than a foot (0.3 m) wide.

In the News

Read all about it! Satellites are front-page news.

Orbiter Spies Robot on Mars

October 6, 2006

NASA today released one of the most striking satellite photos ever taken of Mars. It shows a feature called the Victoria Crater in extraordinary detail. The photo was snapped by the *Mars Reconnaissance Orbiter*. The satellite was passing 168 miles (270 km) above the Martian surface.

The crater is half a mile (0.8 km) wide. Mission managers were thrilled by the photo. It was taken by the most powerful camera ever sent to take pictures of another planet. And they were stunned by what they saw when they zoomed in for a closer look.

There, clearly visible near the crater's rim, was a tiny NASA rover. They could even make out its tracks in the sand. "It's one of the most [amazing] images I've ever seen," said the rover's lead scientist, Steve Squyres.

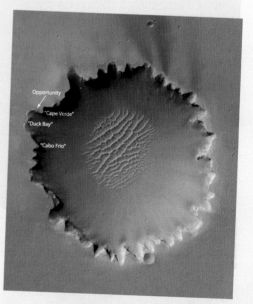

Victoria Crater as seen by the *Mars Orbiter*. By zooming in on the photo, scientists were able to spot the *Opportunity* rover.

The *Mars Reconnaissance Orbiter* travels in a low orbit that takes it over the Martian poles. It completes an orbit in fewer than two hours.

Opportunity, as it's called, is one of two rovers exploring Mars. It landed there in early 2004. The robotic explorer was designed for a three-month mission. But it's still going strong after almost three years.

The *Mars Reconnaissance Orbiter* is just starting its mission. It traveled 310 million miles (499 million km) to reach the red planet. Soon it will begin its scientific work. The orbiter joins two other satellites that have been circling Mars for several years. But its instruments are far more powerful than theirs.

One of the mission's main goals is to look for signs of water. Water is a key ingredient for life. And scientists know that there is water on Mars. They also know it once had much more water. Where did that water go?

The orbiter will also monitor the daily weather and study the planet's rocks. And it will be looking for landing sites for future missions. "We're looking for that sweet spot, where we can go down with other instruments and look for evidence of life," said project scientist Richard Zurek.

For now, the only sign of life on Mars is the presence of robotic explorers from Earth—evidence of the human creativity and skill that designed them.

Space Junk

There's a lot of stuff up there. And most of it is junk.

As the art on these pages show, it's getting crowded in space. About 40 countries have launched satellites since *Sputnik*. Today, there are about 9,000 objects bigger than a softball orbiting Earth. About 1,000 of those are working satellites.

Most of the other 8,000 objects are space junk. The biggest pieces are dead satellites, rocket parts, and metal fragments from exploded spacecraft. There are lots of nuts and bolts. There's even some garbage from a Russian space station that no longer exists.

How do we know? The U.S. Space Command keeps track of what's up there. Its electronic eyes can see something the size of a basketball 600 miles (966 km) away.

All that debris is dangerous to working satellites. So engineers are looking for ways to clean it up. In the future, engineers may use space tugs to collect old satellites. Or they might shoot laser beams at them to change their orbit. The junk would fall toward Earth and burn up in the atmosphere.

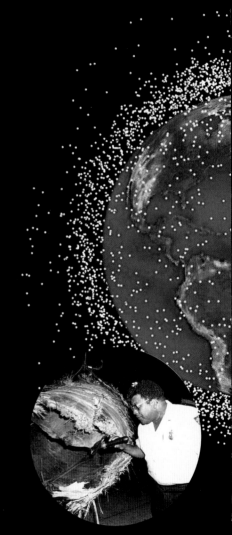

Hunk of Junk

A customs official inspects a large piece of *Skylab* found in Australia.

Vanguard 1

The oldest bit of debris is *Vanguard I*, the second satellite successfully launched by the U.S. It's been in orbit since 1958. This spacecraft was so tiny that Soviet leader Nikita Khrushchev described it as "the grapefruit satellite." It has circled the globe almost 200,000 times.

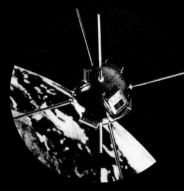

Skylab

Some objects in low orbit do fall back to Earth. Most burn up before they hit the ground. *Skylab*, the first American space station, fell to Earth in 1979. (There were no astronauts on board.) Some of it fell into the Indian Ocean. Other pieces landed in western Australia. Nobody was hit, but the town of Esperance fined the U.S. $400 for littering!

Dangerous Debris

Bits of space debris damaged this solar panel from a satellite. Objects in orbit travel at high speeds, so they can cause a lot of damage. "We get hit regularly on the [space shuttle]," says Joseph Loftus, an engineer from NASA. "We've replaced more than 80 windows," he says.

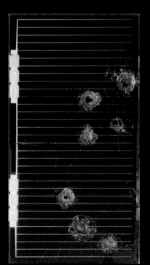

51

HELP WANTED:
Space Mission Director

Are you fascinated by satellites? Here's more information about the field.

24/7: You manage several missions at the National Aeronautics and Space Administation (NASA). Tell us about the THEMIS satellites, which were launched on February 17, 2007.

DR. JENKINS: This is the first time NASA launched five identical satellites on a single rocket. [They will go] on a two-year journey to unravel the mystery behind . . . substorms in [space].

24/7: What are substorms?

DR. JENKINS: Just as hail and tornadoes accompany the most severe thunderstorms, substorms accompany the most intense space storms. Understanding and predicting space weather is important to ensure the safety of spacecraft and astronauts.

24/7: Were you there when THEMIS was launched?

DR. JENKINS: Yes! I had my own monitor and headset on in the launch control room. Launches always provide an unexplainable thrill, seeing a mission you spent years on developing being placed in space. I attend all my launches. It is always hard to believe that I am doing what I dreamt about.

24/7: How did you get interested in science?

DR. JENKINS: I was interested in science before I was seven years old. I use to conduct experiments around the house with car batteries. At one point my room was totally battery operated. I also enjoyed fixing things around the house. My mother predicted that I would be the first man on the moon but Neil Armstrong beat me out.

24/7: Do you still wish you could go to the Moon?

DR. JENKINS: In some respects. But my job allows me to develop satellites that help [people] on Earth and in space. I enjoy making contributions for the betterment of [humankind].

24/7: What advice do you have for young people who are interested in a career in science?

DR. JENKINS: Never stop dreaming. Dreams help individuals to set goals to achieve. Also, young people should try to shadow people in the field of interest if at all possible. Look for programs such as internships in the field. Look for mentors, people who you know that can provide advice. Also, be a mentor to a younger person. Pass on your own skills and enthusiasm.

Dr. Willis S. Jenkins is the Explorer Program executive in the Science Mission Directorate at NASA Headquarters.

DO YOU HAVE WHAT IT TAKES?

Take this totally unscientific quiz to see if working with commercial or spy satellites would be a good career for you.

 Are you good with details?
a) I always see things that no one else notices.
b) Sometimes.
c) Are you kidding? Not until I trip over them.

 Have you ever snooped around someone's house?
a) Yes. I like to see if their bedrooms are messy.
b) I've considered taking a quick peek.
c) Never. That's terrible!

 Do you know what an engineer does?
a) Chemical, electrical, industrial, or mechanical? Or aerospace?
b) They use technology to solve problems, right?
c) You mean the guy who drives a train?

 Do you keep up with new gadgets and technology?
a) Of course. It's amazing!
b) I'm only interested in stuff that's useful to me.
c) I tune out when friends talk about electronics.

 Are you interested in how things work?
a) Definitely. I once fixed our toaster. And our lamp. And our computer.
b) Sure—if someone shows me.
c) I need help putting batteries in the remote.

YOUR SCORE

Give yourself 3 points for every "**a**" you chose. Give yourself 2 points for every "**b**" you chose. Give yourself 1 point for every "**c**" you chose.

If you got **13–15** points, you probably have the right stuff to become a satellite expert.

If you got **10–12** points, you might be good at working with satellites.

If you got **5–9** points, you might want to look at another career.

1
2
3
4
5
6
7
8
9
10

HOW TO GET STARTED...NOW!

GET AN EDUCATION

▶ Take as many math and science courses as you can. Also take courses in photography, computer science, and environmental studies.
▶ Start thinking about college. Look for schools that have good engineering, communications, computer science, environmental studies, and space science departments.
▶ Graduate from high school!

STAY INFORMED

▶ Read the newspaper and visit news sites online. Satellites of all kinds are often in the headlines. Keep up with what's going on in science, technology, and world affairs.
▶ Go the library and get books about satellites and the space program, the environment and weather, computers, and photography.
▶ There are many great Web sites about space, satellites, and espionage. Check out the NASA, SPACE.com, NGA, and CIA sites.
▶ Take a look at the books and Web sites listed in the Resources section on pages 56–58.

It's never too early to start working toward your goals.

GET AN INTERNSHIP

▶ Look for an internship with an engineering group, photography studio, or satellite TV company. If you live near a NASA facility, try to go on a tour. Ask lots of questions.
▶ Or visit one of the many air and space or science museums around the country. If you live near one, call and ask if you can do volunteer work there.

LEARN ABOUT JOBS IN THE FIELD

There are lots of jobs that relate to satellites and espionage. They include:
▶ Aerospace, electrical, and mechanical engineer
▶ Telecommunications technician
▶ Computer scientist
▶ Software developer
▶ Imaging or mapping specialist
▶ Intelligence analyst
▶ Mission controller

Resources

Looking for more information? Here are some resources you don't want to miss!

PROFESSIONAL ORGANIZATIONS

Central Intelligence Agency (CIA)

www.cia.gov
Office of Public Affairs
Washington, DC 20505
PHONE: 703-482-0623
FAX: 703-482-1739

The CIA was created in 1947 when President Harry Truman signed the National Security Act. The organization works to collect information that will help keep the United States safe. It also engages in research and development of high-level technology for gathering intelligence around the world.

Federal Bureau of Investigation (FBI)

www.fbi.gov
J. Edgar Hoover Building
935 Pennsylvania Avenue, NW
Washington, DC 20535
PHONE: 202-324-3000

The FBI works to protect and defend the U.S. from terrorism and foreign threats. It also upholds the criminal laws of the U.S and provides leadership for federal, state, and local law enforcement.

National Aeronautics and Space Administration (NASA)

www.nasa.gov
Suite 5K39
Washington, DC 20546-0001
PHONE: 202-358-0001
E-MAIL: public-inquiries@hq.nasa.gov

The mission of this organization is to pioneer the future in space exploration, scientific discovery, and aeronautics research. The headquarters of NASA are located in Washington, D.C., but the agency has offices in Florida, Texas, and many other states.

National Geospatial-Intelligence Agency (NGA)

www.nga.mil
Office of Corporate Relations
Public Affairs Division, MS D-54
4600 Sangamore Road
Bethesda, MD 20816-5003
PHONE: 800-455-0899

The agency analyzes spy satellite information and provides reports to the U.S. government.

National Reconnaissance Office (NRO)

www.nro.gov
Office of Corporate Communications
14675 Lee Road
Chantilly, VA 20151-1715
PHONE: 703-808-1198

The NRO designs, builds, and operates U.S. reconnaissance satellites. It is staffed by members of the Department of Defense and the Central Intelligence Agency.

WEB SITES

CIA Kids' Page
www.cia.gov/kids-page/index.html

This site gives a great overview of what the agency does.

IMINT Gallery
www.fas.org/irp/imint/index.html

This site has actual spy satellite images for you to check out.

International Spy Museum
www.spymuseum.org

The International Spy Museum in Washington, D.C., is a great place to learn more about spy satellites.

NASA THEMIS Mission
www.nasa.gov/mission_pages/themis/main/index.html

This site is devoted to the THEMIS mission. It even includes a movie trailer and video on the mission.

National Air and Space Museum
www.nasm.edu

The National Air and Space Museum is part of the Smithsonian Institution. It's home to some of the world's first satellites!

NGA Kids Page
www.nga.mil/ngakids/intro.html

It looks like a comic book, but it actually gives a good idea of what the NGA does. If you want career information, go to www.nga.mil and click on "careers."

Today's Military
www.todaysmilitary.com

This site has loads of information about military careers. If you're interested in spy satellites, a military background can help.

BOOKS

Fridell, Ron. *Spy Technology*. Minneapolis: Lerner Publications, 2006.

Gaffney, Timothy R. *Secret Spy Satellites: America's Eyes in Space*. Berkeley Heights, N.J.: Enslow Publishers, 2000.

Johnson, Rebecca, L. *Satellites*. Minneapolis: Lerner Publications, 2006.

Kupperberg, Paul. *Spy Satellites*. New York: Rosen Publishing Group, 2003.

Spangenburg, Ray. *Artificial Satellites*. New York: Franklin Watts, 2001.

Sweetman, Bill. *High-Altitude Spy Planes: The U-2s* (War Planes). Mankato, Minn.: Capstone Press, 2001.

Walker, Niki. *Satellites and Space Probes*. New York: Crabtree, 1998.

[Satellite Bite]

Eighteen-year-old Paul Dickson saw Sputnik in the night sky. In his book, *Sputnik: The Shock of the Century*, he writes, "Watching Sputnik [cross] the sky was seeing history happen with my own eyes. . . . I was electrified, delirious, as I witnessed the beginning of the Space Age."

A

aerial (AIR-ee-uhl) *adjective* from the air

allies (AL-ize) *noun* people or groups that are on your side

arms race (armz race) *noun* a competition between nations to accumulate or develop the most weapons

atmosphere (AT-muh-sfeer) *noun* the mass of air surrounding Earth

B

bugged (bugd) *adjective* describing a phone line or a location that has a secret listening device attached to it or planted in it

C

capsule (KAP-suhl) *noun* a small compartment on a spaceship

chemical weapons (KEM-uh-kuhl WEH-puhnz) *noun* weapons that are made of deadly poisons and gases; they can kill a large number of people at once

CIA (see-eye-AY) *noun* an agency of the U.S. government that deals with foreign intelligence (the secrets and knowledge of other countries) and counterintelligence (misleading spies from other countries). It stands for *Central Intelligence Agency*.

civil war (SIV-uhl war) *noun* a war between opposing groups of people within the same country

Cold War (kold war) *noun* the period after World War II when communist countries, such as the Soviet Union, and noncommunist countries, such as the United States, were competing against one another

communist (KOM-yoo-nist) *noun* describing those who believe in communism, a system that says all property is owned by the government

D

democracy (dih-MAH-kruh-see) *noun* a type of government that is run by its people, who elect their leaders

dictator (DIK-tay-tur) *noun* a ruler who has complete control over a country; dictators do not have to answer to the people and can treat them any way they want to

E

eject (ih-JEKT) *verb* to push something out

espionage (ESS-pee-uh-nahzh) *noun* the act of using spies to gain information about the plans and activities of other groups

eyewitness (iye-WIT-nuhss) *noun* a person who saw something happen

G

GPS (jee-pee-ESS) *noun* a system that uses satellites to track and locate people and objects on Earth. It's short for *global positioning system*.

H

HUMINT (HYOO-mint) *noun* human intelligence, or information gathered by secret agents or spies

I

IMINT (IH-mint) *noun* imagery intelligence, or getting information from satellite photos or other kinds of images

informants (in-FOR-muhnts) *noun* people who supply agents and other officials with secret information

intelligence (in-TEL-uh-jens) *noun* secret information gathered by spies about another country's military and political operations

intimidation (in-tim-uh-DAY-shun) *noun* the act of making threats to scare people

M

missiles (MIH-suhlz) *noun* weapons that are launched to strike something at a distance

mustard gas (MUHS-terd gas) *noun* a deadly gas that causes blisters and then makes its victims bleed inside their bodies

N

NASA (NA-suh) *noun* a U.S. agency that leads space exploration. It is short for *National Aeronautics and Space Administration*.

nerve gas (nurv gahs) *noun* a gas that attacks the human nervous system, including the brain

NRO (EN-ar-oh) *noun* an organization that designs, builds, and operates reconnaissance satellites. It is short for *National Reconnaissance Office*.

nuclear weapons (NOO-klee-ur WEH-punz) *noun* missiles and other weapons armed with nuclear material that can cause incredible damage

O

orbit (OR-bit) *noun* the path of a satellite around a planet, moon, or star

R

reconnaissance (ree-KAHN-uh-sahns) *noun* the secret scouting or exploration of an area, usually for military or political purposes

resolution (rez-uh-LOO-shun) *noun* the measure of how clearly and in how much detail you can see a photo

S

satellite (SAT-uh-lite) *noun* a natural or human-made object that circles a planet, moon, or star

SIGINT (SIG-int) *noun* signal intelligence, or gathering information by intercepting communications such as radio and phone transmissions

solar system (SO-lur SIS-tuhm) *noun* the sun and all the planets and other natural objects that revolve around it

Soviet Union (SO-vee-uht YOON-yuhn) *noun* the former government of present-day Russia and surrounding countries

spy (spye) *verb* to work in secret to get or send important information

T

technology (tek-NOHL-uh-gee) *noun* the use of science and engineering to do practical things, like build better machines

transmit (transs-MIT) *verb* to send a message or radio signal from one place to another

U

United Nations (yoo-NY-ted NAY-shuns) *noun* an organization made of representatives from all over the world. It is abbreviated as *U.N.*

W

WMDs (DUH-bul-yoo-em-deez) *noun* chemical weapons like nerve gas that can kill many people at once. It's short for *weapons of mass destruction.*

Index

CONTENT ADVISER: Steven Aftergood, Director of the Project on Government Secrecy, Federation of American Scientists

Intelsat V, a communications satellite that broadcasts information to all areas of the world.